HOOKHAM POETRY LIBRARY

VOLUME I

Sandra J. Hookham
&
Thomas E. Hookham

Hookham Poetry Library
Volume I

Copyright © 2011
All rights reserved worldwide

For information about permission to reproduce selections from this book write to:

Permissions, Multeity Books
E11403A West Norwegian Valley Road
Ontario, WI 54651

To order additional books visit:

https://www.createspace.com/3600541

ISBN

13: 978-0615484396
10: 0615484395

Printed in the U.S.A.

Multeity Books

OTHER BOOKS
by Sandra J. Hookham

(Children's)

Concepts Of Time Series

Midnight to Noon = Noon to Midnight

illustrated by
Barbara A. Hookham

To order visit:
https://www.createspace.com/3514449

COMING IN 2011

Hours to Days & Days to Years

illustrated by
Barbara A. Hookham

To order visit:
https://www.createspace.com/3596649

Our Past, Present, & Future

illustrated by
Barbara A. Hookham

To order visit:
https://www.createspace.com/3596654

(Adult Novel)

Lisa's Triumph
Victory Over Leukemia

co-authored by
Patricia D. Sullivan

with
Dr. Rolv K. Slungaard M.D.

To order visit:
https://www.createspace.com/3596483

Analytical Political Poetry (Vol. I)

To order visit:

https://www.createspace.com/3603975

Hookham Poetry Library (Vol. II)

To order visit:

https://www.createspace.com/3603010

(Children's)

Children's Stories in Rhyme
(Book 1)

illustrated by
Barbara A. Hookham

To order visit:
https://www.createspace.com/3600542

COMING IN 2012

(Young Adult Novel)

The first in a series

Quiet Breeze

illustrated by
Barbara A. Hookham

To order visit:
https://www.createspace.com/3600544

(Adult Novel)

RENVERSEMENT

To order visit:
https://www.createspace.com/3605413

Poems that rhyme
Are remembered most;
Look back through time
From coast-to-coast,
And quickly you shall surely find
These are the best of every kind.

Hookham Poetry Library
Volume I

Contents

Sharing the Gift of Life	*Sandra J. Hookham* ... 1
Dust Covered Ambrosia	*Sandra J. Hookham* ... 5
It's Today So Remember	*Sandra J. Hookham* ... 13
Wake Up	*Thomas E. Hookham* .. 14
Cabin Fever	*Sandra J. Hookham* ... 16
Spring Fever	*Sandra J. Hookham* ... 21
Paths to Reservations	*Sandra J. Hookham* ... 25
Profanity	*Thomas E. Hookham* .. 29
Issues with Issues	*Thomas E. Hookham* .. 30
To Us	*Sandra J. Hookham* ... 32
Greed	*Sandra J. Hookham* ... 34
Walk in my Shoes	*Sandra J. Hookham* ... 35

Contents Continued

Borrower's Fate	*Sandra J. Hookham ... 36*
Santa Came Early	*Sandra J. Hookham ... 38*
Success	*Sandra J. Hookham ... 42*
A Cheater's Rap	*Sandra J. Hookham ... 44*
Little Bear Beware	*Sandra J. Hookham ... 46*
<u>Se Plaire</u>	*Sandra J. Hookham ... 52*
Missing You	*Sandra J. Hookham ... 53*
Secrets	*Sandra J. Hookham ... 56*
Searching	*Sandra J. Hookham ... 58*
Sun-Drenched Enchantress	*Sandra J. Hookham ... 61*
The Dog Bar	*Thomas E. Hookham .. 91*
So Bad—So Good	*Sandra J. Hookham ... 92*

DEDICATED TO THE
SULLIVAN FAMILY

Lisa

Pat

Tom

Doug

Jeff

Dave

Sharing the Gift of Life

Lisa—whose name means Consecrated to God:
Surely you have earned that right
While so near death you bravely trod,
And now with open arms invite
The world to know about your fight.

Five long years this battle raged
That doctors once thought none could win,
And higher stakes were never waged,
Nor fonder hands absolved of sin,
Than those between you, the Lord, and kin.

A family that stood close by your side—
When you needed them, they were there.
You saw the tears your mother cried;
You felt the love...the tender care,
The trust and faith you all could share.

A cherished life was nearly lost:
A child with so much still ahead.
Somewhat dearly you paid the cost,
Yet angry words were seldom said
And bitter tears quite sparsely shed.

Despite all suffering, you clung to life
—Expunging the fears that shackled your heart—
Enduring the pain, the doubt, the strife;
Sadly you watched rainbows and innocence depart,
As your delicate dreams elusively fell apart.

A childhood stolen from your path—
Its many pleasures torn away...
With amazing tolerance, you show no wrath,
Only kindness in the things you say.
This is what you give today:

Sharing the Gift of Life

A hand that leaves the fingerprints of hope
Upon the lives of all you touch;
A perception unveiling the way to cope,
And support to which we firmly clutch
When hardships seem to weigh too much;
Footsteps that carry us away in time,
To find the bliss among life's sorrow—
Up great mountains you help us climb,
And from your faith we gently borrow
The courage to face each new tomorrow;
Eyes that behold the treasures around them;
Ears that enfold the sounds of the earth;
Lips that speak of this precious gem—
The God-given life we receive at birth,
And arms that entwine its precious worth;
A voice so sweet and soft and low,
It hides the presence of silent cries;
And though your face ostends a glow,
Somewhere far behind those eyes,
Still lurk the memories they disguise.

The battle scars you must carry,
Even healthy years cannot erase,
For the hands of time can never bury
And leave behind without a trace,
The occasional gloom that drifts across your face.

Wrapped in a cloud of family love,
Surely, Jesus now holds your hand;
Certainly, you have been blessed from above
—A miracle child, before us you stand—
Kissed by angels upon this land.

Your words like pillars hold promise high
And plant the seeds of faith beneath our fears,
Yet swallowed within, rests a muffled sigh—
Unshed and noiseless are the blinked-back tears
That linger still from tragic years.

~ Sandra J. Hookham

DUST-COVERED AMBROSIA

My eyes tight shut are reviewing the past
As I drift through this night on a sleepless cloud,
Where memories from childhood are with me at last,
Blanketing my thoughts in a vivid shroud.

I can lightly skip through time and space:
Nearly touching a dear one whose soul is now gone;
Glimpsing *each* wrinkle on a kind, loving face;
Even hearing the words to which I was drawn.

More often that not, my thoughts come to rest
In a big old house—many miles from home—
Where those red-letter weekends were always the best,
Allowing me time and the freedom to roam.

Each room billowed forth with its own luscious smells;
They cling to my senses like cobwebs in trees...
Where the air rushing through gently lifts and swells,
Before stealing them off to float with the breeze.

I recall the steamy aroma of home-baked bread,
Flooding from a table which still smelled of wood...
Where Grandma covered it with a linen spread,
Fondly tucking in corners to make a chafing hood.

My mouth faintly waters as I delectably dream
Of that good canned meat in those big glass jars,
Or milk in a jelly glass—that's yellow with cream—
For washing down old-time snickerdoodle bars.

Whether winter or summer, it still held its charm
—In the sparkling bright sunshine or glitter of snow—
As Grandma would say while lightly holding my arm,
"Now Petty, be careful! And watch where you go."

Dust-Covered Ambrosia

Gingerly off to the barn I would romp:
Breathing the balm of corn and loose hay;
Or the pungent, sweet silage the cows loved to chomp,
While for oats and molasses the horses would neigh.

Springtime let lilacs fill the misty air,
And around them tulips would sway and hover
Over lilies of the valley so white and fair...
Caressing the lawn with their boutonniere cover.

Then later, the peonies sprang out like a flame,
As did wild verbena across the land;
Flushed in crimson and blushed with rouge they came,
Dancing pompously forth like a bright marching band.

Back in the house when supper drew near,
I might accompany Grandfather off to the cellar...
Where the earth's spongy dampness I remember so dear,
As I stood by the side of that whiskered old feller.

We'd bring up some jars full of rutabagas or corn;
That trap door in the floor they'd lower down tight;
Then a table with cowslips I'd carefully adorn,
While sniffing their fragrance with all of my might.

Later on in the evening, I'd examine each room:
From that spicy pantry with a creaky, worn floor
—All through the upstairs of its wallpapered womb—
Till I made my way back to the kitchen once more.

There I'd refresh by the water pail's weeping shine,
From a long-handled dipper fashioned in tin;
The taste of the water—slightly soft—was so fine,
As it dripped from my lips and rolled down my chin.

While twilight melted the shadows away,
The elders would savor their steaming coffee;
And I...in another room would play,
As they sipped and chatted ever so softly.

Dust-Covered Ambrosia

I poked all around—every place I recall:
From a mothballed trunk in that cedar closet,
To horse magazines garnering the stairway hall;
As I fondly bethink, each left some binding deposit.

Bygone treasures seen from that high-backed couch,
I still ponder and enjoy as if they were mine...
Like some fragile glass beads in a satin pouch,
Or those taffeta draperies all dripping in shades of wine.

Here, crocheted doilies and hairpin lace,
Like tatted spreads and braided rugs,
My mind's eye—with a clinging embrace—
Ties the knots that a heartstring tugs.

Out from the wall stood a potbellied stove,
With silvery filigree so burnished and grand...
While the wood on the floor made a chestnut trove,
In a mixture of incense that was pleasantly bland.

Slipping through a curtain, into their chamber I came;
An appliqued coverlet neatly scalloped the bed;
Its downy soft mattress and squiggly frame
Had shining brass knobs at foot and head.

The dresser I see cloaked with trinkets and bottles...
While porcelain handles and solid oak base
Are so far removed from the frippery it coddles,
Or the handmade flowers in that sugar-spun vase.

The redolent mixture of lingering perfume
—Like seductive vapors from utopia cast down—
Hung in the closeness of that one-windowed room,
Forming its haunting bouquet for a crown.

Each corner entrusted something familiar, yet new:
From a knickknack shelf gently rounding one angle,
To that old iron crib brushed in periwinkle blue,
While the light barely caught its fading spangle.

Dust-Covered Ambrosia

When bedtime drew near, I'd return aloft...
Where the crackling wood of a nighttime fire
Left a faint trace of smoke to rise and waft,
Like the slippery shadow of a flexible wire.

Clambering to bed, I burrowed in cozy
Under a patchwork quilt or soft feather tick,
To think of that day that had been so rosy,
And how its reflections in my mind would stick.

Drawing a deep breath, my gaze stared blank...
While off in some niche, I vaguely recall
A vintage wood cradle—as beneath the keepsakes it sank—
Imparting an era **"I"** couldn't remember at all.

Then before closing, tempted eyes would seek out
—Through tiny florets and faded nosegays—
Tattered clefts in the wallpaper where plaster peeked out,
Silhouetting faint images in that phantom haze.

Such memories may tickle the senses...
Leaving behind a definite yearning,
To cross back over those vanishing fences
That time and neglect are slowly burning.

But remember this and keep in mind—
Tomorrow, today will have gathered some dust,
And the smiles of the morning will soon fall behind
The shadows of remembrance in which we trust.

Like soft rose petals or sweet lilac scent,
You savor each whiff, but the taste is forbidden...
While those things beyond touch—with deepest repent—
In an unending space will always be hidden.

~ Sandra J. Hookham

IT'S TODAY SO REMEMBER—

IT'S—

>Good when someone leaves their mark,
>
>Great we all possess some spark,
>
>Of talents beaming bright and new—

TODAY—

>When troubles glare through the dark,
>
>And we wantonly wish to disembark,
>
>For rewards at times seem scattered and few.

SO—

>If you think the race is run,
>
>That battles now have all been won,
>
>And future dreams might well escape you—

REMEMBER—

>For some the world has just begun,
>
>And nothing that is said and done,
>
>Counts so much as what you've yet to do.

~ Sandra J. Hookham

Wake Up

You say you quit school at the age of sixteen;
It all seemed so boring and the teachers were mean.
Something's wrong with the system, they can't blame you.
Are you glad you left? Now what will you do?

You quit your job at the place you work.
Yea, the labor was hard and the boss was a jerk;
The hours were long and the pay was low.
Are you glad you left? Now where will you go?

You learned to make a living outside of the law.
It was easy money, but with just one flaw;
You ignored all the lessons you had been taught,
And sooner or later you're gonna get caught.

Wake Up

You got off with probation, but you felt abused;
You forgot all the people you stole from and used.
Then you met a girl who would love you for life,
But only because you had to, you made her your wife.

A family of three is hard to support;
Your wife took a job as a last resort.
Blame the world, there's no job you wanna do.
Wake up quitter! It's not them, it's you!

—*Thomas E. Hookham*

Cabin Fever

The driving snow rapidly reaches its crescendo,
Propelled to the earth by a swirling madness,
While we observe through and ice crusted window,
The velocity and strength which created such sadness.

It's difficult to perceive how life can survive,
Watching the birds as they shiver and tremble,
How the small and the weak will ever contrive,
And for mating in spring again will assemble.

Once it has ceased there's beauty it's true,
As the blizzard subsides and the squall settles down,
And the fortunate ones catch a cozier view,
While the creatures without see the ominous brown.

Cabin Fever

Peaceful adornment covers most of the death,
But leafless trees whisper a fateful reminder,
Of those who perished and drew their last breath,
Waiting for days when the winds would grow kinder.

So here we are trapped in our world of warm,
With little to do but grow tensely perturbed;
On pins and needles we sweat out the next storm,
While our minds and nerves become sorely disturbed.

We turn short with each other and extremely bored,
From this mounting anguish and sad depression,
As the things which we say are often ignored,
In a crude, nasty way by sarcastic rejection.

Some argue and bicker at the drop of a hat,
Being vulgar, cross-grained, and very contrary;
In wild-eyed fury like a grown up brat,
They obscenely threaten till it's really quite scary.

Practically exhausted from being such jerks
—And feeling remorse by a very slim margin—
We humble ourselves with apologetic shirks,
Then justify everything with an ill-tempered jargon.

Eventually, all and sundry settle back to their rut,
Refraining from stuffy and pompous actions,
Behind the windows which must always be shut,
And gazing around at the dismal attractions.

As we peer from the house to the garden so bleak,
Having naught to show save the sunflower's bent heads,
They stand in their row like parishioners—cheek to cheek—
Praying for summer and new flower beds.

In gazing beyond to the forests and hills,
It's hard to distinguish the ground from the sky;
The gray meets the white thus lacking in frills,
Except where the trees stand vertically by.

Looking out across the cold florescent night
—When days are short and gloom prevails—
Where the moon is full making darkness bright,
As through its depth she peacefully sails.

Oh, how we long for those warm summer rains,
Bright flowers of spring, and the limitless greens
—When winter grows warmer and finally wanes—
Allowing such lush, and lavish scenes.

Cabin Fever

But that all seems so distant and far away
—Trying to remember those hot, starry nights—
When the skies keep so overcast, dull, and drab gray,
With the sun and the clouds gripped by constant fights.

So tucked in the cabins away from it all,
Lounging like old folks in soft rocking chairs,
We sit and we stare at the ceiling and wall,
Pondering our troubles and worries and cares.

The majority of people would love to go out
—To a party, a dance, or just get together,
Laughing with friends and frolicking about—
But sadly enough, it's all stopped by the weather.

Events are so few that are planned for the winter,
Yet in summer they conflict and occur back to back;
Wouldn't it be nice if they were spread out just a splinter?
Then, later on in the year there wouldn't be such a lack.

There are a few projects to keep someone busy:
Like cleaning and varnishing, or painting and such.
But most must wait till summer's great tizzy,
For the strong, choking fumes are simply too much.

The three months of summer are brief and curtailed:
For the sun slips away beyond a distant horizon,
While Jan., Feb., and March blow in ne'er hailed,
And bury the ground for to lay our sore eyes on.

Some winters are merciful and others severe,
But even the gentle create ruin and rack,
As the snowflakes appease the cold and the clear,
With this veil of white that seems so black.

Then surprising enough and quite belated,
The days lengthen out to curb cabin fever;
A few weeks of mud make us quite aggravated,
But at last fragrant blossoms will start—Spring Fever.

— Sandra J. Hookham

Spring Fever

Spring fever starts with the earliest thaw,
The first thunderstorm and a clear blue sky,
And though the nights remain fierce and raw,
We're reminded again that summer is nigh.

The weather's still chilly and unpredictable at best,
With snow-flecked days carried in by the wind.
"But that jes' encourages 'n' adds to the zest,"
Remarked the old optimist as he smiled and grinned.

Before very long—if you look toward the clouds,
The geese you'll observe on their northern flight;
They gather in flocks like people in crowds,
And as they V-out, they're an awesome sight.

The frost finally leaves and settles the mud,
As the rains drift in from warmer skies,
And the sadly bent branch produces its first bud,
While sweeter days, the sun tenderly implies.

The days will grow longer with gentle breezes,
Bathed in the soft golden gleam of a radiant sun,
And each living thing its warmth so pleases,
From the dew-sparkled morn till each day is done.

All shall enjoy the sultry mists of a blue-gray deck,
As they sprinkle down from their oven in the sky,
And the year's first rainbow will arch its long neck,
Before the mellowing haze waves a final good-bye.

This life-giving moisture sends down its sweet dressing,
To all that rejoice in the cleansing rhythm,
For the weeping heavens cry out in angelic blessing,
Toward everything living whose praise be with 'em.

Soon, tiny spear-like shoots begin popping up,
Displaying their feathery and fragile green,
Upon the leaves so edged in scallop,
And reflecting a silvery, yet emerald sheen.

Spring Fever

Of course flies and bugs must return to the air,
But with them appear cardinals, canaries, and robins,
While joyously gathering these meals for to share,
As they creep from rocks or their dried corncob inns.

The spring is alive with colors untold,
From the rose's red hue to the daisy's white petal,
Like the violet's deep purple or the buttercup's bright gold,
They all stand out in gay and fine fettle.

But they can't hold a candle to the woodpecker's head,
The densely rich plumage of the oriole,
The teensy hummingbird's throat of red,
Or even the crow who's black as coal.

For mixed with the colors of these brilliant birds
Are the voices of ecstasy and warbled content,
And like throngs of angels vibrantly singing their words,
They mingle together under the sky's blue tent.

Every age-old species reproduces anew:
All plants and animals of the garden we call earth;
From the seeds of last year, they merged and grew
In that summer's jubilant and rapturous mirth.

Each new life must seek its own destination,
While lost in the tide of abundant replenishment,
And though carried away by time and creation,
Will spring forth once more from winter's entrapment.

The earth becomes active with its newfound treasures
—Each blade of grass seems to wriggle and squirm—
Enjoying the splendid and bountiful pleasures,
From the biggest oak tree, to the tiniest worm.

~ *Sandra J. Hookham*

PATHS TO RESERVATIONS

*Many, many decades now reversed,
"We the people..." feebly put ashore,
Trembling ships from seas accursed,
With tattered sails and rats galore.*

*Each drew an icy, mournful breath
For rations gone and malady to show,
Appearing doomed to certain death
In winter's barren bungalow.*

*But then a man so strong and kind
—Standing proudly—called us brother,
And by his fire we warmly dined,
Accepting largess from another.*

We ate his food to give us strength,
Even quaffed strong medicine for ills,
Wholly dependent through winter's length,
And viewed the rewards that help instills.

But we learned no lessons I'm afraid
—From those compassionate and selfless ways—
For we did scoff and laughingly upbraid,
While plundering their sunlit turquoise days.

We robbed this land and pushed them out,
Stripping its resources and killing the game,
Then from booms of ridicule—a victory shout,
To hide the squander and the shame.

Gone by our rash and thoughtless vows
Are those massive forests of pine,
That once combed the air with richly scented boughs,
Leaving it clearly pure, vital and benign.

Paths to Reservations

In their stead rise fallow stones
And scattered prickly ash,
Where tempest-charged winds dry out the bones
That roaring floods did smash.

A promise was granted to the Ojibway—
That if their tribesmen now behaved,
Upon this land they might stay
And not to reservations be enslaved.

Naive and sad they trudged along:
Believing the pledges that were given;
In search of kinsmen who did us wrong,
Since once again they were being driven.

They have their reservations now,
Where the land is harsh and rough,
As we have ours, while heads we bow,
And listen to voices that cry, "Enough."

But down through history one thing is for sure,
And like it or not we all know it is true,
That things never stay quite the same as they were—
That the earth and her children must begin life anew.

The pendulum of time takes a mighty swing
To right the wrongs that have been done
—To change the course of freedom's ring—
And the backward thrust has just begun.

So please be patient my sovereign friends,
For there is good in every race;
You know the strongest tree is the one that bends,
And things will change by God's good grace.

The white man's greed took this land
By deceit and brutal attack,
Yet "Indian Gaming" extends a welcome hand—
And the white man's greed will give it back.

~ *Sandra J. Hookham*

PROFANITY

Did you know that the use of profanity
Dates all the way back to the start of humanity?

Passed down through time and generations,
Across the waters through all the nations—

The compact vehicle in which we ride,
That only small minds can fit inside—

Its user is lacking the imagination
To give something an original presentation.

From the lowly street bums to upper society,
All men use it to vent their anxiety.

Can we stop a language from being precocious
By forbidding the words that sound atrocious?

Ban the obscenities—but others will take their place,
And new dirty words are still a disgrace.

It seems like an insect resistant to spray,
Mutating itself and cascading away.

I guess the curses we'll all have to live with,
And hope the Almighty above will forgiveth.

—*Thomas E. Hookham*

Issues with Issues

The word issues is being overused:
I am issuing this report in hopes you'll be amused.

In some contexts issues and problems mean the same;
If you try to sort it out, you're playing the issues game.

I was issued a ticket for rolling through a stop;
I guess my driving issues did not impress that cop.

I have issues with my teeth and issues with my hair,
Proving I can have issues with things that are not there.

In a recent issue of her lady's monthly book,
My wife read an article that put me on the hook.

Issues with Issues

Things your man should do was the issue that it raised;
Nothing was on the list for which I could be praised.

I had financial issues—no one would issue me a loan;
So I issued a bad check—now I have no phone.

She issued ultimatums which I must surely heed,
Or she will take the house—I'm looking for the deed.

I had issues with my dog who had issues of his own,
So I had him put to sleep and now I am alone.

Please do not judge any man by his basic issues,
Unless you have bravely walked a mile in his-shoes.

—*Thomas E. Hookham*

To Us

Barroom Dear—
Ol' pal o' mine,
Where I might gayly dine,
Upon strong liquor, or just beer,
That waits within its stein.

Happy times,
I know will come;
To us—my loyal chum,
As in my ears, the ringing chimes,
Say, "Make my body numb."

To Us

So, off I drift
To realms unknown;
My logical mind has swiftly flown,
And in the gap, there is a rift,
From which I might softly drone.

But, in morbid fear
My face turns gray,
Like smoke that's curling up away,
Into this hazy atmosphere.
"Please—don't let me puke!" I pray.

~ *Sandra J. Hookham*

Greed

So alike are we to the greedy dog,
Who—with bloated belly—lies beside his bones;
We anguish in regret and mournful dialogue,
While he possesses only agonizing groans.

Being pathetic but true and by far the worst,
Afraid to entrust the tiniest sparrow,
For water—now—he does sadly thirst,
And the bird must want for the marrow.

~ Sandra J. Hookham

Walk In My Shoes

I know they'll never fit just right,
For one is higher and a little tight,
Accommodating this brace upon my thigh;
But, close your eyes and move slowly along,
And hear the birds as they warble a song,
Counting how many by wings that flutter by.

Feel the grass so soft and smooth,
As it tickles your ankles and begins to soothe,
The dreaded fear of being alone and lost;
Then, picture the blossoms on a nearby tree,
As the honey-sweet fragrance drifts off so free,
While beside you some petals are gently tossed.

You cannot peek or the spell is broken:
Just hear the sounds that are never spoken;
Then, grope for the presence of raindrops refined;
Allow your subconscious to drift toward the skies;
And now dear friend you've seen through my eyes,
Because though they are open, I am blind.

~ *Sandra J. Hookham*

Borrower's Fate

Repossession is the gift of law
—Held by tightly bound wrappings
And securing all trappings—
With a slippery ribbon that only the rich may draw.

A poor man must grovel and grope
—Willing out his triumphant intentions
While overlooking all bitter dissensions—
And prove to the opulent, he can smile and cope.

But the funds have a price and they come dear
—For the sorry soul who must sadly sign,
Putting his name and earnings upon the line—
As the meaning of payback looms out very clear.

Like a lord in his castle, the lender gloats down
—As if to vaunt, "I'm better than you
And without my help, what would you do?—"
Then, he soberly squints and grins with a frown.

Borrower's Fate

And should plans turn awry
—With the ball in his court,
Leaving the whole situation about to abort—
Misgivings return, for it's now do or die.

Then a comedown of that formidable day
—When the deadline is now;
No more time will the law allow—
For it goes back if you fail to come up with the pay.

You're taxing your body, your soul, and your worth
—Depriving yourself of the pleasures of life
And creating within suck monumental strife—
Thus, casting away all contentment and mirth.

It's all for these chattels so needed and dear
—By the owner to have and enjoy,
Like the gratis of a baby's pull toy—
But, always the string remains in the rear.

~ Sandra J. Hookham

Santa came early

The countdown was on and the kids were all smiles;
Christmas was coming to fulfill their desires.
Saturday we'd be traveling across many miles,
Visiting relatives...as the season requires.

Friday was Christmas and nothing could stop it:
The gifts were all bought and hidden away;
Our bubble was growing and nothing could pop it;
The cookies were baked...everything was okay.

There remained just one gift that couldn't be wrapped:
That big Barbie House I'd worked on for weeks—
Off in the bedroom where hours I'd spent trapped
Away from kids' questions and wondering peeks.

Santa Came Early

I prefabbed each wall—even put in a sink;
The windows and casings had long since been done,
And the tiny tub and stool of pink
Graciously looked up at a mirror that would stun.

The plan was all set—it couldn't fail;
We would put it together on Christmas Eve.
An hour or so with hammer and nail,
And under the tree it would be ready to leave.

Then a phone call came and to our surprise,
We'd be expected on Christmas—on Friday this year—
Not the day after as you might surmise...
Oh, such joyous and Christmassy cheer.

Just four days to go and we were to be
Away at my in-laws on Christmas Day.
Cards were all mailed and we'd decorated the tree,
"But what of that house?" I thought with dismay.

And the kids were all worried and very upset,
"How will Santa Clause know where he should go?"
Our once happy house began to stew and fret,
And I thought to myself, "Ho...ho...ho!"

We ran in circles for a day and a half,
Going instantly crackers and pulling our hair;
At times the walls echoed a thin, brittle laugh,
But except for bananas, our fruit baskets were bare.

Then, a letter to Santa we hopefully sent:
Begging this favor...that he might come
—Just one day early before we went—
Bringing nice presents and leaving us some.

Yes—Santa came early upon our request.
He did us this kindness as a special treat:
Packed up those toys and gave us the best,
While I hurried to make that doll house complete.

The fireplace was painted all fancy and bright,
Overlooking thick carpets of brown and gold;
Tiny horses were placed on the mantel that night,
Their color of bronze erupting so bold.

But the upstairs and roof just wouldn't fit,
So I attacked it now with square and bevel.
My screws were all loose and I couldn't do spit:
By now...Ma was tilted half a bubble off level.

Santa Came Early

It soon came together with Dad's help of course,
About three in the morning...kids would be up by five!
But I found it could be done with brains not force,
And we were finally ready for the day to arrive.

~ *Sandra J. Hookham*

Success

Noteworthy creations are collected in waves,
Allowing vague images time to develop;
The mind must be tuned so it keenly behaves,
Around the masterpiece it will sagely envelop.

When a standstill is met, let it go for a while;
Fresh returns can bring new-found reflections;
Never permit it to entrap, deceive, or beguile,
The inspiration which conjured up such selections.

Some time must be given for quiet, deep thought,
Whether pacing the floor or clutching the clouds,
Since creativity is not easily wrought,
From yattering with others or by dint of crowds.

Success

Just hold the clock and look around:
Study the abounding colors and shapes,
From turquoise sky to the ornamented ground;
Pry beyond those smooth and deceptive capes.

Each new rock spawns its own special face,
If you delve deep in the twisted details;
And the wonders within, it will rigidly encase,
Unless you seek out those elusive entrails.

The wonders observed on this joyous quest,
Will set in your mind for time eternal,
As the melding creations reveal their zest,
With a flowering blush so pure and vernal.

— Sandra J. Hookham

A Cheater's Rap

The rival love is always known
To the ones who must condone,
And makes the minutes a crawling hell
To those who staidly bear it well.

Between the love and racking hate,
Of a discontented mate,
Never so fine a line was drawn,
Until at last the passion's gone.

A Cheater's Rap

How ironic that when you care,
The love you found is just not there,
And sadly beholding the one mistreated,
It's really yourself that you have cheated.

So grieve the bitter taste of rue,
Your partner gone with someone new,
'Cause everything was just one-sided;
Like a rented flag, your heart's divided.

How can it be that some should fall
Into a love they can't recall,
Or care so little for one who does,
Alas! Grasping for love that never was.

— Sandra J. Hookham

Hookham Poetry Library—Volume I

Little Bear Beware

Padding along on a stranger's path
And sniffing the cool mountain air,
There came one day to this part of the woods,
A tiny cub, black bear.

But, sadly no mother was by his side
To give him love and care,
So now he tries to make it alone,
And for himself must fare.

Little Bear Beware

Not long ago his brother and he
Had made a happy pair,
As through the forest they'd leaped around
With joyous games to share...

Roguishly scrapping or frolicking nimbly,
From whence to here to there,
And close behind to keep them safe
Came the mother bear.

Then one day as they drowsily rose
From their cozy little lair—
Shuffling along through the trees,
She tripped across a snare.

She struggled and fought and lurched about
Till her nostrils began to flare,
Only managing now, to wear herself out
And her cubs to frighten and scare.

They helplessly watched when men came by
Who filled their hearts with terror;
Three shots rang out that echoed a silence,
changing her brown eyes into a glassy stare.

Then limply she collapsed
Without a chance or prayer,
And no more would they be followed
By the mother bear.

In his wild and crazy flight
Of horror and despair,
The absence of his brother,
This cub was not aware.

And when at last he stopped to rest
With foam upon his hair,
He looked around and sadly found
His brother was not there.

Little Bear Beware

To venture back and look for him
He knew he did not dare,
For in the distance again was heard
That deafening rifle's blare.

Solidly frozen for a moment,
So afraid to make an error,
But now a whisper urged him on,
Like that of mother bear.

And so he pushed forth once again,
Although he knew not where,
Seeing cruel and frightening things
All new and strange and rare.

Within his sad and lonely self,
He knew he must prepare
To conquer his dismay,
And travel on elsewhere.

Trudging along, he noticed his paw
Had been cut in a nasty tear—
Bleeding hard and painfully sore,
It needed some time to repair.

When it finally healed,
A scar he'd always wear—
To remind him of this terrible day,
And mighty awesome scare.

He'd never forget the sound of the gun,
Or the smell of his mother's slayer,
Or how he was forced to jump and run
With the quickness and fright of a hare...

For he knew deep down within his heart
The chase could not be fair;
His life and blood, the stalking hunters
Would never ever spare.

Little Bear Beware

He's been a giver and a taker,
A goer and a stayer;
He used his cunning every day—
Like wisdom born of an old soothsayer.

And though the many years became
A soft and kind conveyor
Of easy times and healthy days,
His fur now grows a little grayer.

— *Sandra J. Hookham*

From the novel Renversement

*Se Plaire

Roll like the tumbleweed drawn by a wind,
But leave me never dead to honor—
Your motor a horse so refined and thin-skinned,
With silky-wet harness draped upon her.

So channel me forth on hooved, flightless wings
—As the whipping jib of a full-rigged schooner—
While your sleek-set mane vibrantly sings
To usher me home just a little sooner.

— *Sandra J. Hookham*

*Se Plaire (French) to please one another; to be content

From the novel Renversement

Missing You

Last rites were given by the priest,
And your spirit's been released;
Although your body is deceased,
My love for you has still increased.

When we were young our life seemed vast,
But looking back—it went too fast;
We knew of course it could not last,
And now our dreams are in the past.

We shared a love that steadily grew,
Molded uniquely for me and you;
Within its grasp our hearts were true,
Clinging together to see us through.

Missing You

In trying to do what we should,
Sometimes the bad outweighed the good.
No one's perfect—that's understood;
We lived each day the best we could.

You left my home a lonely place—
And in my heart an empty space;
But in my dreams we still embrace,
Restoring a smile upon my face.

— Sandra J. Hookham

Secrets

A secret forged with someone true
Is less than a secret known only to you.
Keep your secrets all untold,
Until you've gotten very old...

For a secret shared with even one,
May someday be kept from truly none,
And a secret shared with two or more,
Won't be a secret anymore.

When one man finds out others have heard,
He thinks you won't know who spread the word;
Your secret will be taken to the wind,
Around the world and back again.

Secrets

And when your secret comes back to you,
A little different and misconstrued,
You'll want to know, "Who set it free?
How could a friend do that to me?"

Don't look far for one to blame —
It is you who wears the shame,
'Cause you're the one who misjudged the friend
That brought this secret to its end.

— Sandra J. Hookham

From the novel Renversement

Searching

Someday one who finds this flask,
Hidden deep within its cask,
Searching further—then will ask,
"From what purpose comes my task?"

As underneath this bleeding heart,
You begin to play the part,
Finding destiny to end and start,
While everywhere, my thoughts will dart.

Searching

Here's a treasure you behold,
From these ashes dead and cold,
As the meaning will unfold,
And bring symbolic, buried gold.

Trace your footsteps to that bed,
Neath the spot where laid my head,
Below a floor you've yet to tread,
And pull the tiny, zippered thread.

Now it's there within your grasp,
As you unlock a bolted hasp,
This magic lantern you might rasp,
Or simply loose the buckled clasp.

To reap its worth you must unbind,
A message in those lines entwined,
Study slow—with open mind,
And catch the words that lie refined.

Please renown the stolid sight,
And its ghost in fearless flight,
For the crown of fresh delight,
Blazes in this morn from night.

~ Sandra J. Hookham

Sun-Drenched Enchantress

She has golden hair
Streaming down upon the land,
And bright blue eyes
Engulfing all remaining sky;
Her skirts unfold...
Most colorful and grand,
Sequined—throughout—
With life that passes by.

Abundantly flowering
Beneath those dazzling gleams...
Orange, red,
And woolly banksia dance
—Resurrected by
Such delicately jeweled dreams—
Across her smoothly undulating,
And broad expanse.

And so many kinds of orchids
Upon her bosom blooms
—In dainty elegance—
Like that of bearded, sun, or fleshy lip,
Whose petals rise in purple, white,
And pinkish plumes,
Giving summons to
The burgeoning flush of hyacinth and cowslip.

Across her showy flounces,
Sprinkled grasses cling:
From yellow clumps of kerosene,
Or spinifex called porcupine,
To feathery kangaroo,
And nut grass by the "mound spring,"
And the lemon-scent lingers,
While desert cane bristle in her sunshine.

The antipodean climate
Of this land down under,
Modestly harbours within her
Dry and squelching heat—
An island continent,
Which creates a mystic wonder,
Of treasures man will not so quickly ruin
Or deplete.

Sun-Drenched Enchantress

From the Macdonnel Range's
Classic Organ Pipes—
To those wavy ribbons of banded cliffs
At Ormison Gorge,
Where purple, white, ocher,
And red form horizontal stripes,
As the winnowing rains and sands of time
Relentlessly scourge.

Here, in a unique valley
Grows the cabbage palm,
Found nowhere else
Upon her captivating land.
And whispering cycads
Murmur their prophesying psalm,
Like waving seaweed
Reflecting promise from the sand.

Red-backed kingfishers and rainbow birds
Are gliding past,
While white-faced herons
Silently stalk for fish,
Out among the reeds
Of deep, dark pools that contrast;
These are the glorious colors
Of her rocky dish.

There are stands
Of the cream-flowered bloodwood tree,
And rocky slopes
Studded by cone-shaped cypress pine,
While spinifex—resembling a wheat field
In its yellow sea—
Come to mingle
With the range's spread of pink-flowered verbine.

This lady of the present
Holds within her past,
Secrets of existence
On a sun-baked earth:
Where salty lakes and river beds
Are sprawling dry and vast,
Waiting for the silvery rain
To usher in rebirth.

Some colossal channels
Look strange and very full of...
Intricate impressions
—Resembling microscopic cells—
Like Amadeus Lake
When viewed from far above,
Where, on crusty dregs
This giant likeness dwells...

Sun-Drenched Enchantress

Or Lake Callabonna,
Whose abstract canvas is besmeared
With black and green,
And streaked by white,
Where salt beds
Glitter an ancient beard,
Atop this prehistoric
Graveyard site.

From endless billows
Within her "outback,"
Of the "bush"
And great "red heart,"
Where the land
Will dry and crack,
And stones of eons
Break apart—

To white-capped mountains
In Victoria,
Where snow gums
Drip of varnished ice;
They're fully clad
In sprigs of green euphoria,
With leaves so graceful
As to entice...

The gentle breezes
From below,
Or sparkling rays
That steadily shine,
To bring a warmth
And evening glow,
While siphoning drinks
From nature's stein.

The Blue Mountains
—A shining haze of eucalyptus oil upon them—
Watch the eucalyptus flowers
Serenely rest,
Displaying yellow stamens,
And orange-red bulb and stem,
And gum leaves
With which the galah prefers to line its nest.

These galah birds are easily observed
—Loud and bright—
A variety of raucous parrot
Called the rose-breasted cockatoo;
Each manifesting hues
Of pink and gray and white,
They liven up the treetops
With frenzied clamour and to-do.

Sun-Drenched Enchantress

Then, away up in the north
We're scanning,
Beckoned off
To Queensland's mighty cliffs,
Where giant trees
The air is fanning,
As through their boughs
It gently lifts.

Springing in clumps,
From the dark forest floor
Abounds
The red-stemmed green kangaroo paw;
Its flowers
Are so strangely unusual in shape and color;
Such uniqueness
Of red, black, and green sculpturing they draw.

Here, the aura lies
Sweet and damp—
Sprinkled from
Her weeping eyes,
Below the shimmering
Of her lamp
As she expires
In willful sighs.

Then from the ocean
A priceless boon,
Created upon
Its salty wing—
She receives
Her gray monsoon,
And all the flowering
It shall bring.

This land of intrigue
—So gloriously dressed—
Whose national flower
From the wattle tree looms,
Drenching her landscape
From east to west,
With a Midas touch
Of golden blooms.

Here dwell the platypi,
And red-eyed crocodiles;
They are the lagging remnants
Of a distant past
—Like spiny anteaters,
Or highly peculiar reptiles—
Creatures time forgot
Is how they may be classed.

Sun-Drenched Enchantress

She's nobly clad—from rock-bound coast
To sparkling azure hems—
By legions of distinctive growth
That form her living frills;
Above these patterned slippers
Rise whispering, giant gems,
Smiling down
On mountains, plains, and meager, rolling hills.

She yields treasured forests:
Of jarrah, karri, and blackbutt;
While offering rosewood, mahogany,
Pine, and tallowwood;
Even some varieties
Of gum and beech are cut;
Like her blackwood,
Red cedar, tulip and sandalwood.

Tee trees weep from yellow blooms
A honey-sweetened scent,
Mingling with the chemical tang
Of nearby mineral pools;
Graceful palm trees
Mould their light green tent,
While mountain ash in tiny bouquet
Are her heavenly jewels.

Big, orange-yellow brushes
From the corkwoods waggle,
And gracious flame gums
Lightly bend,
While bower birds
Over nesting ornaments haggle,
Or steel-blue, peregrine falcons
Silently wend.

Whether charmed by those soothing, flute-like notes
Of the butcher bird,
Or inspired from rich, melodious whistles
Of a rufous songlark's trill,
All heads sharply turn,
As the western shrikethrush's piping call is heard
Above silent branches,
While shattering the air so still.

Sassy willie-wagtails
Busily chop about on high,
While pestering
A large, brown falcon on the wing;
And flocking budgerigars,
Like thick, dark clouds blot out a crystal sky,
O'er the cheery, white-winged wrens'
And bellbirds' gentle tinkling.

Sun-Drenched Enchantress

From southern Queensland's
Purling Brook Falls,
To the
Great Australian Bight,
The black swan
And sedge-tailed eagle calls,
While soaring past
In rhythmic flight.

And in-between
There is so much,
Upon those swathing,
Pleated folds;
Her changing mantle
Bending to the touch,
While wind and water
Slowly moulds—

Ranges like
The Macdonnell or Flinders,
So much different
And yet the same:
While one sports life,
The other cinders,
And both have cherished
The storms that came...

Or the gleaming red ruffles
Of a desert called Simpson,
Where
The swirling willy-willys twist and glide
Between
Her parallel ridges of crimson,
That may be almost
As high as wide.

And somewhere near
That burning "centre,"
—Not so far
From Alice Springs—
Her landscape acts
As brilliant mentor,
Revealing secrets
That she brings...

From far beyond
A gibber plain,
Whose polished surface
Of wind-swept stones,
Seldom produces
Life or rain,
As the timeless rocks
She bluntly hones—

Sun-Drenched Enchantress

To oddities like
The Devil's Marbles,
Of giant
Granite blocks so round;
Each chamfered shape
Misleads and garbles,
Where in their valley,
They silently astound.

Suddenly, there stands alone
Upon her distant scope,
A ghostly landmark
—Known to us as Ayers Rock—
With native name Ulura;
Her water holes bring hope,
Welcoming the multitudes
Of many a thirsty flock.

Maggie Springs is but one
—A dark and wet purlieu—
Of eleven totaled,
Where varied throngs collide;
From lizards, birds, and snakes,
To dingo and kangaroo,
They all must meet together
And peacefully abide.

This singular outcropping
Has many changing hues:
From sombre under clouds
To evening's ruddy glow,
For it is the sunlight
From which she takes her cues,
And with the passing shadows
Can alter fast or slow.

The Kangaroo Tail quaintly hangs
Upon one flank,
Where a ribbon of sky
Is brightly peeking through;
Between the slender rifts
Of body and springing shank—
Here, sacred holes of time
Widened and waywardly grew.

And with final,
Curious looks,
We view in awe
That massive Brain;
Its pitted surface
Forming shadow-haunted nooks,
Where erosion stole
Each particle and grain.

Sun-Drenched Enchantress

Then sweeping forth abruptly
—Across this land so flat—
Passing by the spinifex
And shrunken mallee tree,
Where forms the sandy surface
—Her silken welcome mat—
A carpet dressed in splendor
For all the world to see.

Her desert flowers
Offer strong resistance,
To the sterile drought
And constant, parching heat;
In special ways
They clutch to this existence,
With upturned petals—
Her shining face they greet.

Here,
Bloom the desert grevillea's striking orange;
They catch a flaming essence
Of the sun itself,
While cone-like flowers
In clusters do arrange,
The smoldering petals,
So full of nectar there on rounded shelf.

Hundreds of species of mulla mulla
Dot her blushing cloak:
Some waving lavender-gray tufts;
Or bright green, wobbling crowns;
Their fuzzy blossoms
Bursting forth as they awoke;
While others spread the earth
With popcorn batches of white before the browns.

Rains bring out the parakeela's purple carpet
Of jelly-like, whiffling fronds,
Which like the white array of golden-hearted daisies
For water did wait;
And seagulls journey
To Lake Eyre's bountiful ponds,
While black-faced wood-swallows
Flock to the billabongs and mate.

Crawling termites
Build a clay-covered nest
All honeycombed
And of treelike height,
While giant yellow anthills
Spring to the north and west,
And the swollen bodies of honey ants
Get ready for drouth or blight.

Sun-Drenched Enchantress

There are konkleberry trees,
Flying foxes, and fruit eating bats,
Lung breathing fish, butcher birds,
And sugar gliders,
Wolves with pouches,
Carnivorous mice, and native cats,
As well as military dragons,
Bottle trees, and whistling spiders.

Onward to the Olgas,
This reverent journey reaches,
Skimming a faint horizon
For her massive domes
—Where by their breezy shelter
Many a soul beseeches—
To find this Valley Of The Winds
Whose grass she steadily combs.

And by those
Violet-pink old mountains,
Dwell the falcon,
Skink, and hill kangaroo;
They use her rocky pools
For fountains,
Like zebra finches or honeyeaters
Who dot her sky of blue.

This land of Katatjuta
—Which means "the many heads—"
Gives life to Bubia Creek
Beneath that hump Mount Ghee,
Along whose glistening banks
Grow many flower beds,
From yellow rattlepod,
To the red of Sturt's desert pea.

There lies within these waters
A tangle of wild oats,
Down between the graying shards
Of cracked and dimpled walls;
Flowing with her descant runnel,
Nature's bounty floats,
Wrapped safely and secured
By painted, rippling shawls.

Climbing up
This hollow gorge
—Surrounded by daisies
And bushes of mint—
Among the green leaves
Of bloodwood might forge,
Some red-flowered mistletoe
In the sun's fiery glint.

Sun-Drenched Enchantress

Then just around a corner
Of solid, curving rock
—Freckled by dwarf acacia
And native plum and fig—
There lies a hidden place...
Decked in amber frock,
This "Valley of the Mice Women"
In yellow billy button wig.

All these changing regions
Hide far beyond "The Black Stump"
—That fabulous, mystical gateway
To "outback" and wonder—
Where arching leaves of grass trees tower
In a mighty clump,
Surmounted by spiking cattails
Growing loftily asunder.

And most symbolic
Is this affectionate-looking animal—
The cute and timid koala
With leathery nose;
Eating only tender, eucalyptus leaves
To get him full,
Fluffed in rich and velvety fur
He strikes a drowsy pose.

Here,
Pretty face and banded hare wallabies feed,
Along with the flightless emu,
And merino sheep;
And the great grey kangaroos
Abundantly breed,
So fleet of foot
And with stretching leap.

Seldom seen
Is the princess parrot
Who lies like a lizard
Along the tree's stout limb,
Or the hardyhead fish
Locked in their "mound springs" garret,
Where minerals from rising hot water
Deposit a rim.

There's the cracking of whipbirds,
And bush turkey's warbled caw,
The captivating lyre
Who mimics another's noisy stew,
And zebra finches
Sucking up water as through a straw,
Instead of tipping back their heads
Like other birds will do.

Sun-Drenched Enchantress

And birds called little kings
—Who here and there are found—
So bright and orangish-red
With belly and beak of white,
Their ebony tails
Forming tiny medallions round,
From wiry, black feathers
Coiled up so tight.

From Wave Rock
Which curls above a straight track
—Its gargantuan overhang
Of sweeping granite stone,
Resembling a petrified breaker
All streaked in gray and black,
In Western Australia it rises...
So majestic and all alone—

To the "tombstones"
Of the Krichauff Range,
Or the "stone blades"
Of the Warrumbungle Breadknife.
Her surfacing garb
Gives way to great change,
While paving the way
For unique and matchless life:

Like the mouse-sized honey possum
Of the southwestern coast,
Who by use of its needling tongue
And extra long snout,
Loves drawing sweet nectar
From a flowering host,
As do crimson chats—
Birds that walk rather than hop about;

Or hazy colored turtle frogs,
Who with the termites survive,
Existing far from water
As the bustard birds do;
And strange hopping mice
That mange to stay alive
On only the moisture in seeds—
Going without a drink their whole lives through.

From the cackling laughter
Of a bright kookaburra bird,
They say
That one might predict the rain;
And should a snake
Be perilously stirred,
His slithering body
Will be quickly slain.

Sun-Drenched Enchantress

Springtime arouses the purple hardenbergia
And white clematis too;
And here
Beside her sparkling waterfalls, arrive
Scattered clumps
Of rock isotome with pale flowers in blue,
While way out on her sandy plains
The Christmas bells survive.

She bears many rare
And brilliant flowers in the wild:
The rosemary spider
Of hot pink and white is one;
Like waratah,
And native fuchsias here have smiled;
While fringed violets, woody climbers,
And crimson honey-myrtle stun.

Miracles from nature
Will never end or cease:
As the dainty flower of a trigger plant
Begins to sway and rise,
Like a cat's back to the touch
Its stature will increase,
Spreading pollen upon the visitor
Before it slowly dies.

An insectivorous
Indian sundew plant,
Whose white flowers
Exude a sugary glue,
Trapped its victims
To unwillingly grant
The nourishment
From which it developed and grew.

Ah,
But on her eastern border
—Across that
Great Dividing Range—
The rains come ample
And afford her,
A most abundant green
And welcome change.

Here,
The urban populations grew,
To build great cities
From these jungle lands;
Their glorifying voices
Called upon and drew,
A flocking multitude
Of willing and helpful hands.

Sun-Drenched Enchantress

Standing proudly is Sydney,
Whose landmark is the Harbour Bridge:
Capitol of New South Wales,
All cherish her majestic opera house so noble.
Ten roofs curve up
As giant sails billowing on some seaward ridge,
Massive shells like moon-washed pearls—
Though only slightly global.

With the greatest horse race from down under,
Melbourne is her rival city:
Capital of Victoria
And home of the Melbourne Cup.
While national capital of Canberra
Stands apart so pretty,
With Mount Stromlo Observatory
For carefully looking up.

Queensland is
The Cinderella state,
And Brisbane is
Her capital,
While back across
Those rugged mountains wait—
More cities
From beyond her sandy bowl.

Adelaide
—The capital of South Australia—did rise;
Known as the city of churches
Is her fame;
And the Northern Territory's capital
Calmly lies
Way up by the sea
With Darwin as its name.

Called the friendly city
—From across the Nullarbor Plain—is Perth:
Being the capital of West Australia
Upon the good Swan River;
Gateway to Europe, Africa, and India
Is her priceless worth;
And here Kings Park—
A taste of the natural bush will give her.

From spires and chimney pots
To skyscrapers,
From Charles Kingsford's plane
The Southern Cross,
To—
Woomera's Blue Streak rocket launching capers,
The fossickers and gentlemen bushmen
Quickly spread across.

Sun-Drenched Enchantress

All have added
To her history and past,
Some reminders
Of their proud esteem;
Though lifeless bodies are gone,
Their deeds will surely last,
Bringing forth a zesty,
Futuristic dream.

Early on came Gregory Blaxland: crossing
All the mountain ridges—
Descending
To the plains and bush—
Mapping out
Those gapping bridges—
And driving
Exploration's needed push.

Then, came Captain Charles Sturt
And his fearless men,
Opening up
The winding Murray River channels;
And Ernest Giles traversed
Each desert and rocky glen,
While Kennedy tried unlocking
Queensland's jungle panels.

From crooks and robbers
Like Ned Kelly,
Known as
"The man in the tin hood—"
To the first aboriginal hero
Called Jacky Jacky,
Whose deep love and unswerving loyalty
Did a world of good.

Some transformed
Her thirsty face
—Of this searing "outback,"
Sometimes called the "back o' beyond."
Through irrigation
Her sands they grace,
With well-watered grasslands
Or a millionaire's pond.

Here too,
Roam blonde-haired, native aborigines:
Still grinding seeds
Of the nardoo plant;
Performing late night dances
Called corroborees;
And singing on
In solemn, rhythmical chant.

Sun-Drenched Enchantress

From the moving here of
Captain Cook's tiny cottage
In the city of
Melbourne's Fitzroy Gardens,
Or Elizabeth Farm House—
The oldest dwelling of great age,
To where the
Sydney Tower's concrete hardens...

From the
Royal Flying Doctor Service,
To a mining town
Called Broken Hill,
Where unfair laws
Made women nervous,
And kept their husbands
Quiet and still...

From
The Battle Of The Coral Sea,
And to
The Battle Of Midway...
Americans and Australians fought side by side
To keep her free,
And
That is how she'll stay.

So let us not forget
The growth
Of this
Incredible land—
Where aborigine
And white men both,
Together
Must always stand.

— *Sandra J. Hookham*

The Dog Bar

I went to the dog bar to lap up some booze.

All my dog friends were there; I had nothing to lose.

The Boss dog was there to keep us in line;

The wimp dog was there lapping up wine.

Two punk dogs were trying to stir up a fight;

Boss dog quickly sent them running in fright.

The dogs were all wiggling with tails in the air;

I wanted to sniff but only could stare.

Over there is that she dog who gave me fleas;

Never again will I go with that tease.

—*Thomas E. Hookham*

♥

So Bad—So Good

When the breeze
In the trees
Starts to blow
Down the snow,
And the sky overhead
Looks as gray as lead,
And the ice on the pond
In the field over yond
Is thick as a brick
Down by the creek—

So Bad—So Good

When a dead branch breaks
Neath a million flakes,
Or a hollow oak
In its wintry cloak
Starts to creak and crack
From the weight on its back,
And the young elms bend
As they start to blend
With earth and sky
And appear to die—

When the blanket on the hill
Grows deeper still,
And the bushes in white
Sink right out of sight,
And the land looks bare
With no warmth to share,
And nature's breath
Is as cold as death,
And the birds are gone
Like flowers from the lawn—

When the snow on the eves
No longer leaves,
And icicles hang
Like a tiger's fang
By the window sill
In a frosty chill,
But the chimney's smoke
From the fire we stoke
Drives out the storm
And you're cozy and warm—

Then its time
To gently clime
In the nearest bunk
With a handsome hunk,
And forget about the cold
As your arms unfold,
Let the blizzards gust
—Bring on hot lust—
While the fire in your soul
Burns hot as coal.

~Sandra J. Hookham

www.ingramcontent.com/pod-product-compliance
Lightning Source LLC
Chambersburg PA
CBHW071306040426
42444CB00009B/1890